AMAZING ORIGAMI

Origami Space

Catherine Ard

Please visit our website, www.garethstevens.com. For a free color catalog of all our high-quality books, call toll free 1-800-542-2595 or fax 1-877-542-2596.

Library of Congress Cataloging-in-Publication Data

Ard, Catherine.
Origami space / by Catherine Ard.
p. cm. – (Amazing origami)
Includes index.
ISBN 978-1-4824-2267-2 (pbk.)
ISBN 978-1-4824-2268-9 (6-pack)
ISBN 978-1-4824-2204-7 (library binding)
1. Origami – Juvenile literature. 2. Space vehicles in art – Juvenile literature. I. Title.
TT870.A73 2015
736.982–d23
First Edition

Published in 2015 by
Gareth Stevens Publishing
111 East 14th Street, Suite 349
New York, NY 10003

Models and photography: Michael Wiles
Text: Catherine Ard
Design: Emma Randall and Belinda Webster
Editor: Joe Harris
Space images: Shutterstock

Printed in the United States of America

CPSIA compliance information: Batch CW15GS: For further information contact Gareth Stevens, New York, New York at 1-800-542-2595.

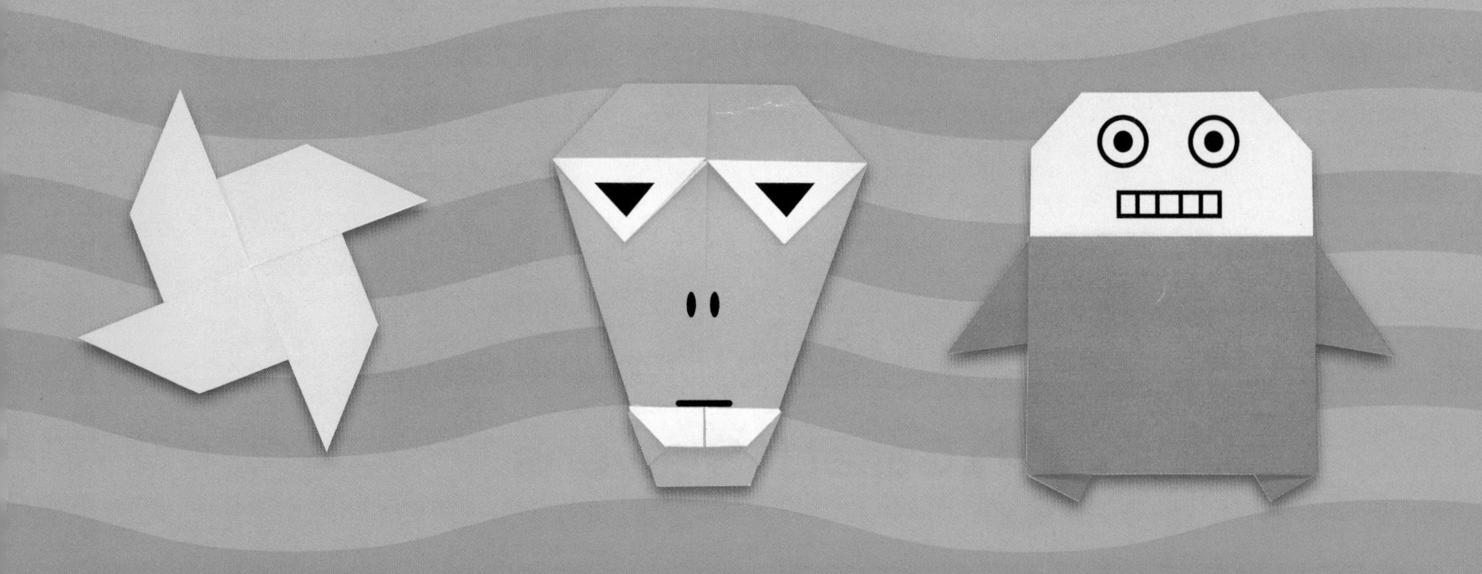

Contents

Basic folds

Origami has been popular in Japan for hundreds of years and is now loved all around the world. You can make great models with just one sheet of paper... and this book shows you how!

The paper used in origami is thin but strong, so that it can be folded many times. It is usually colored on one side. Alternatively, you can use ordinary scrap paper, but make sure it's not too thick.

Origami models often share the same folds and basic designs. This introduction explains some of the folds that you will need for the projects in this book. When making the models, follow the key below to find out what the lines and arrows mean. And always crease well!

KEY

valley fold - - - - - - - - - - - - - -

mountain fold ....

step fold (mountain and valley fold next to each other)

direction to move paper

push ▼

hold

MOUNTAIN FOLD

To make a mountain fold, fold the paper so that the crease is pointing up towards you, like a mountain.

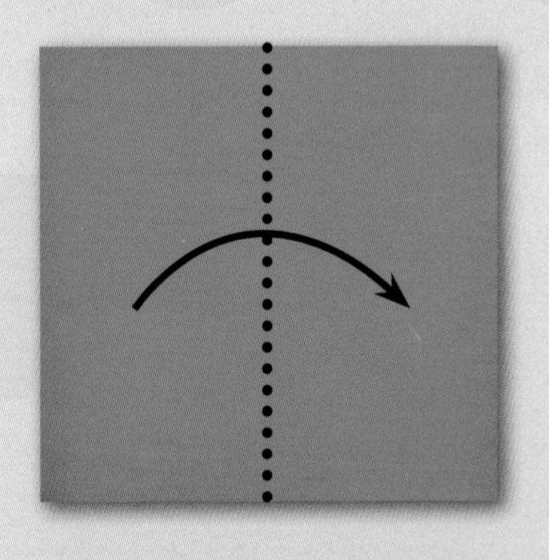

VALLEY FOLD

To make a valley fold, fold the paper the other way, so that the crease is pointing away from you, like a valley.

INSIDE REVERSE FOLD

An inside reverse fold is useful if you want to make a nose or a tail, or if you want to flatten off the shape of another part of an origami model.

1. Practice by first folding a piece of paper diagonally in half. Make a valley fold on one point and crease.

2. It's important to make sure that the paper is creased well. Run your finger over the crease two or three times.

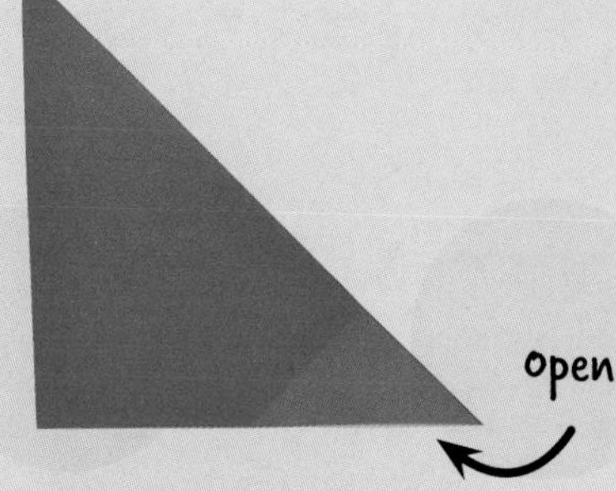

3. Unfold and open up the corner slightly. Refold the crease nearest to you into a mountain fold.

4. Open up the paper a little more and then tuck the tip of the point inside. Close the paper. This is the view from the underside of the paper.

5. Flatten the paper. You now have an inside reverse fold.

OUTSIDE REVERSE FOLD

An outside reverse fold is useful if you want to make a head, beak, or foot, or another part of your model that sticks out.

1. Practice by first folding a piece of paper diagonally in half. Make a valley fold on one point and crease.

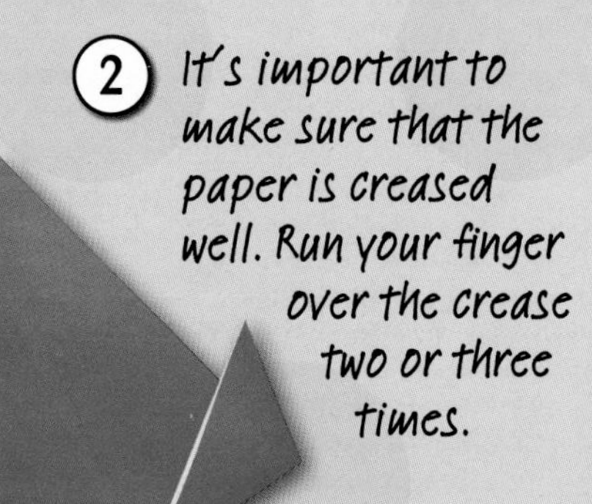

2. It's important to make sure that the paper is creased well. Run your finger over the crease two or three times.

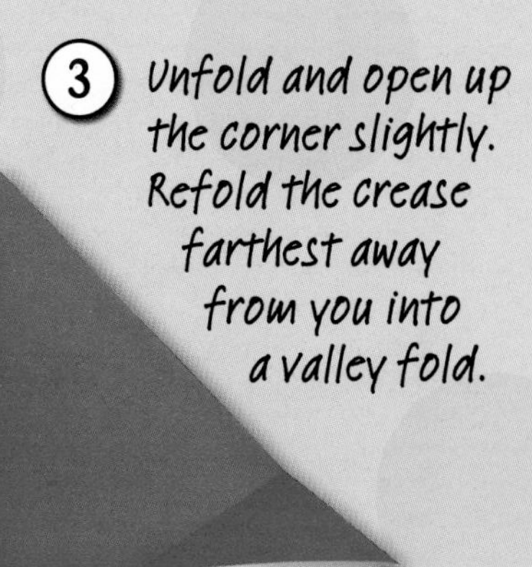

3. Unfold and open up the corner slightly. Refold the crease farthest away from you into a valley fold.

4. Open up the paper a little more and start to turn the corner inside out. Then close the paper when the fold begins to turn.

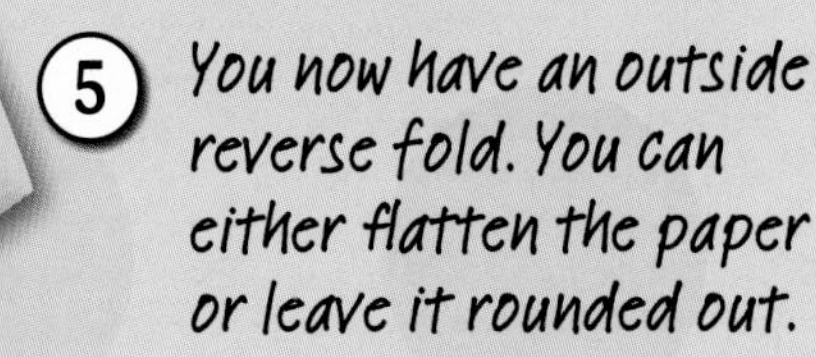

5. You now have an outside reverse fold. You can either flatten the paper or leave it rounded out.

Rocket

Easy

There's a thundering roar as the rocket fuel bursts into flames. 5-4-3-2-1... LIFTOFF! Start your own incredible space mission with this cool origami rocket.

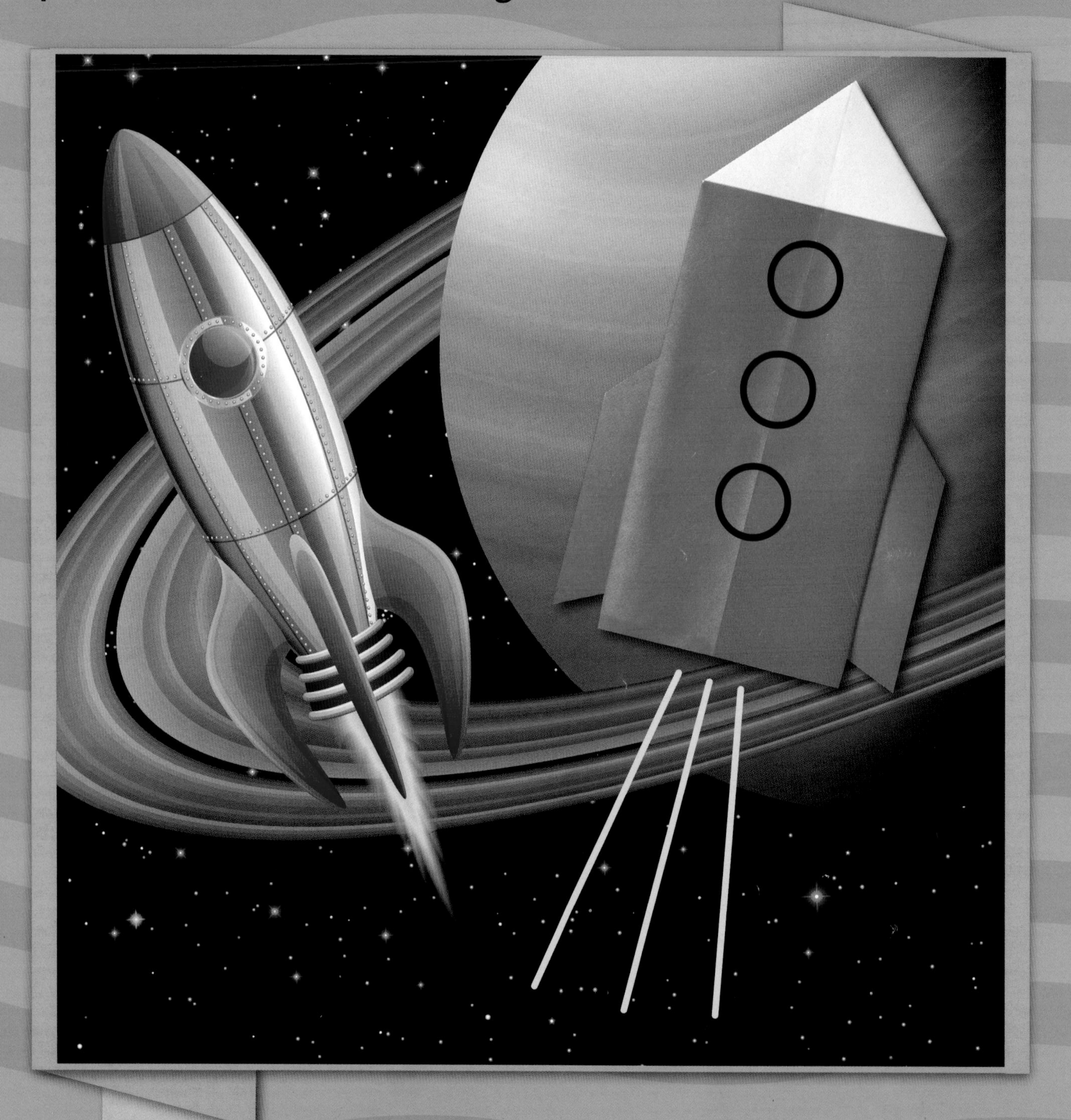

1. Start with the paper colored side up. Fold it in half from left to right and unfold.

2. Valley fold a wide strip along the top edge.

3. Turn the paper over.

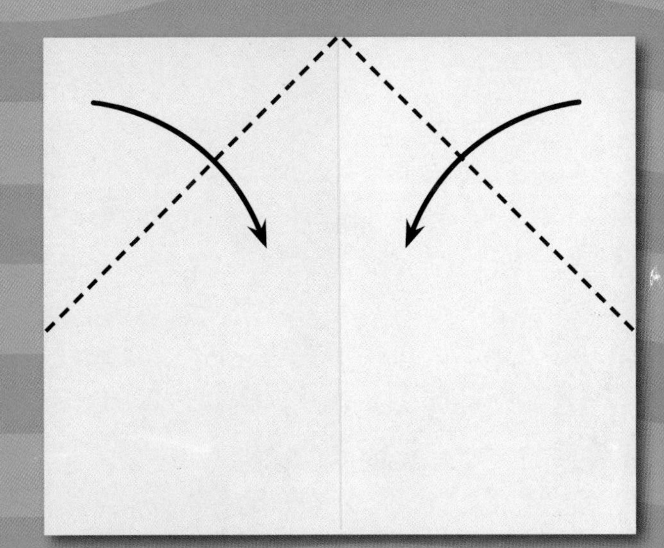

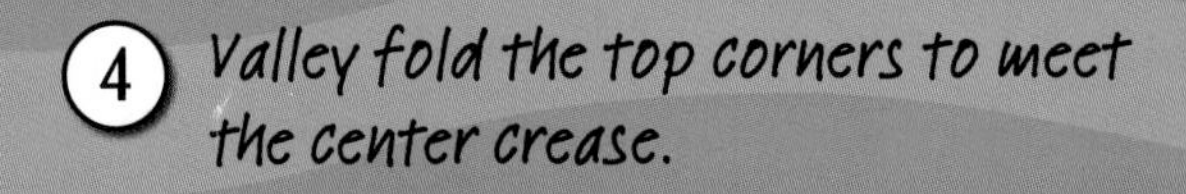

4. Valley fold the top corners to meet the center crease.

5. Valley fold the right side in line with the edge of the colored triangle.

Did You Know?

The first space travelers were animals. Monkeys, mice, cats, and dogs were all sent into space before astronauts.

6. *Valley fold the right side again.*

7. *Now valley fold the left side in line with the edge of the colored triangle.*

8. *Valley fold the left side again so both sides match.*

9. *Open up the inner corner of the right flap and valley fold the top layer.*

10. *Press the paper flat.*

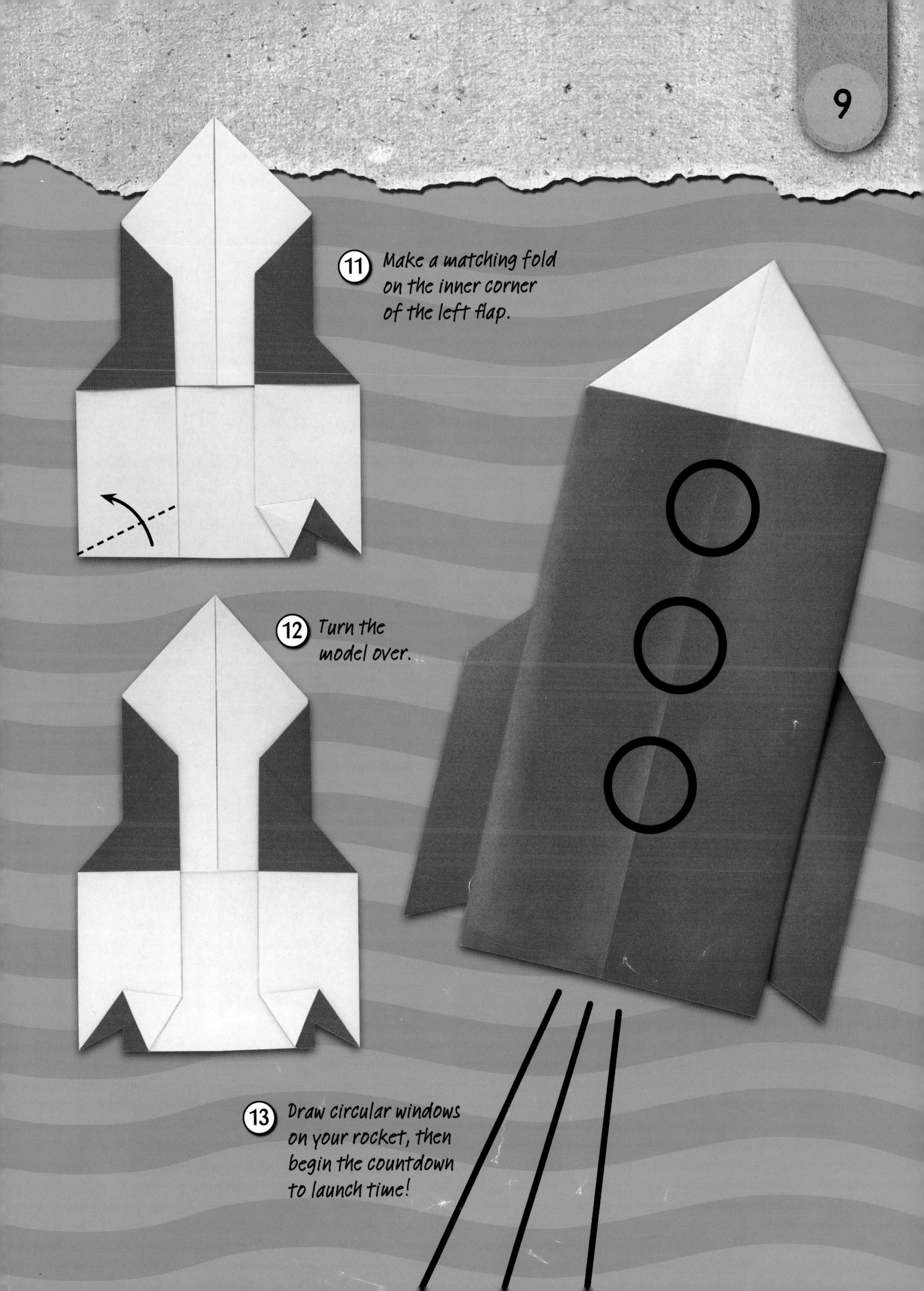

11 Make a matching fold on the inner corner of the left flap.

12 Turn the model over.

13 Draw circular windows on your rocket, then begin the countdown to launch time!

10

Robot

Easy

Whether they are roaming around Mars or collecting rock samples from the moon, robots are perfectly at home in space. Fold this little robot so he's ready to explore a new planet!

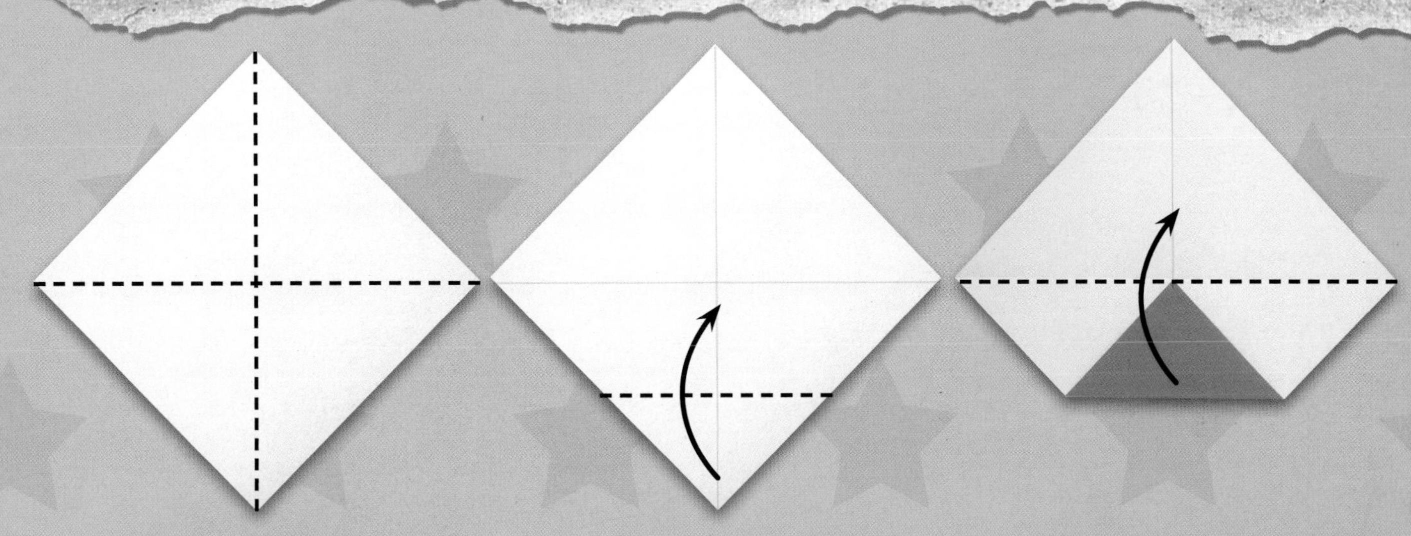

1. Place the paper as shown. Valley fold the paper in half one way and unfold, then the other way and unfold.

2. Valley fold the bottom corner so the point meets the center.

3. Fold up the bottom edge along the center crease.

4. Your paper should look like this. Turn the paper over.

5. Valley fold the left point onto the right side.

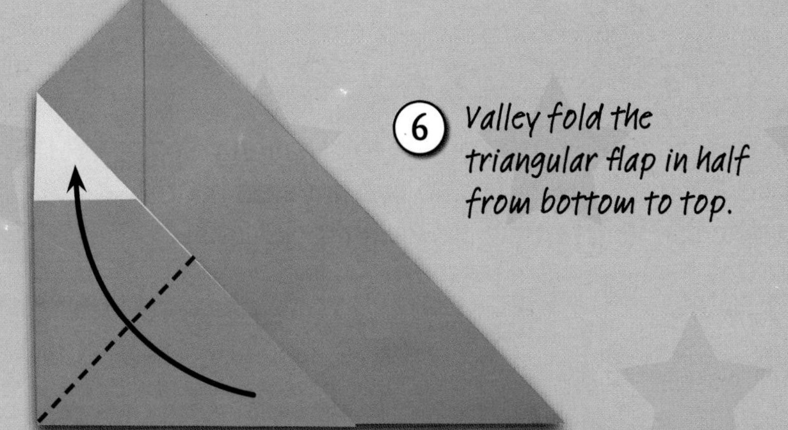

6. Valley fold the triangular flap in half from bottom to top.

7 Fold down the top point of the flap as shown.

8 Now valley fold the right point onto the left side.

9 Valley fold the triangular flap in half from bottom to top.

10 Fold down the top point of the flap to match the other side.

11 Fold down the point at the top.

Did You Know?

Robonaut is the robot used on the International Space Station. He has arms, legs, and five-fingered hands, so he can help out the crew with tricky jobs!

12 Valley fold the tips of the top corners.

13 Fold over a strip along the bottom of the model.

14 Make angled valley folds to the top corners of the strip. These are the legs.

15 Turn your model over.

16 Draw a friendly face on your robot. Now your high-tech helper is ready to head off into the unknown!

UFO

Medium

Could this mysterious spacecraft be carrying alien visitors from distant planets? Choose a dark paper color and fold a flying saucer to hover in the night sky.

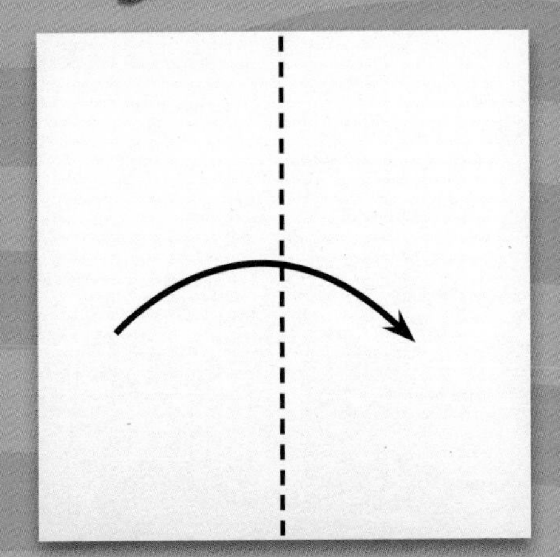

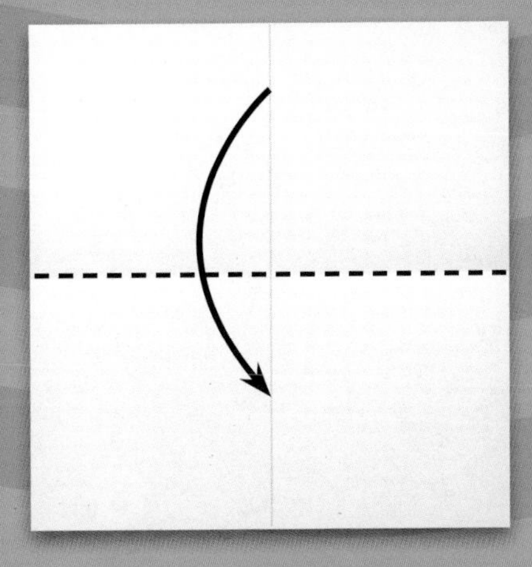

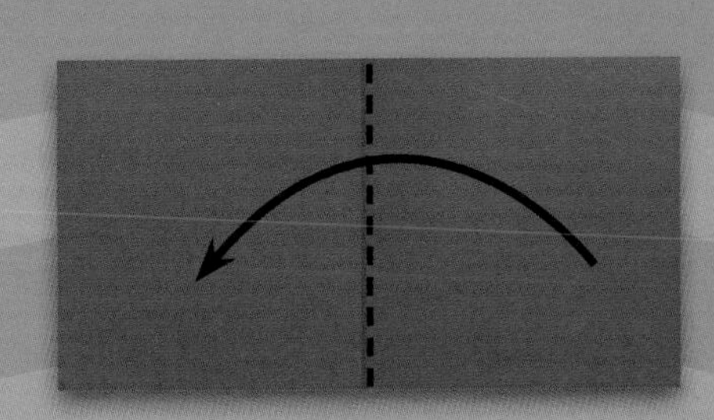

1. Start with a square of paper, colored side down. Fold it in half from left to right and unfold.

2. Fold it in half from top to bottom.

3. Now fold the paper in half from right to left to make a square.

4. Open up the top layer and pull the corner to the right. Press down on the top and flatten the paper to make a triangle.

5. Turn the paper over.

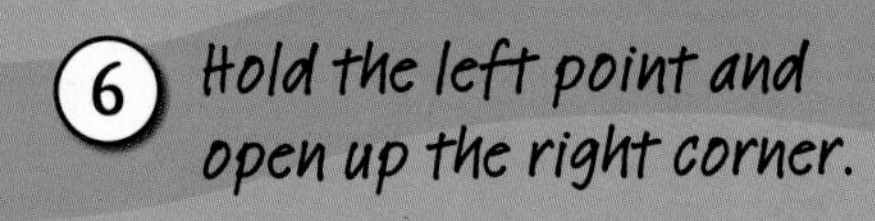

6. Hold the left point and open up the right corner.

OPEN

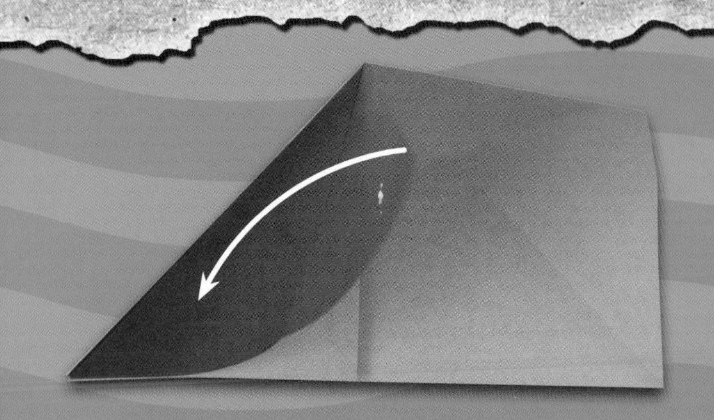

7 Pull the top layer over so that the corner meets the left point. Flatten the paper to make a triangle.

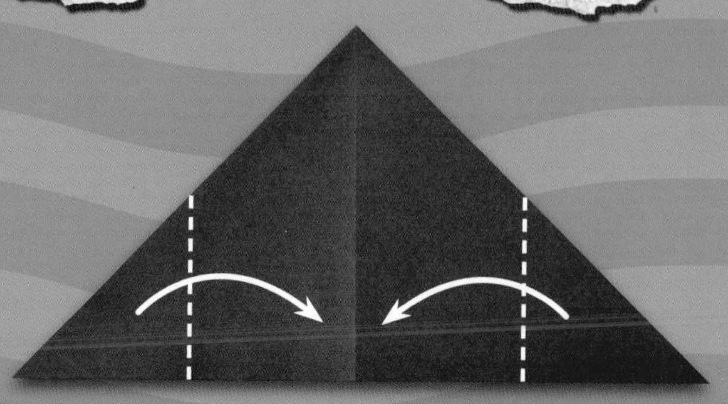

8 Valley fold the top layer of the left and right points to meet on the center crease.

9 Valley fold the right flap so that the outside edge lines up with the inside edge. Unfold and open up the point, then flatten it into a kite shape.

10 Do the same on the other side. These are the jets for the UFO.

Did You Know?

In 1947, a pilot saw nine UFOs in the sky. He said they moved like saucers skipping on water. The name "flying saucers" has been used ever since!

11. Make a step fold across the center of the model.

12. Fold in the tips of the points.

13. Turn the model over.

14. Draw a row of round windows to finish the spacecraft. Now your UFO is ready to beam up some earthlings!

Galaxy

There are billions of galaxies in the universe, each one made up of billions of stars and planets. Use some yellow paper to fold this spiral of brightly glowing stars.

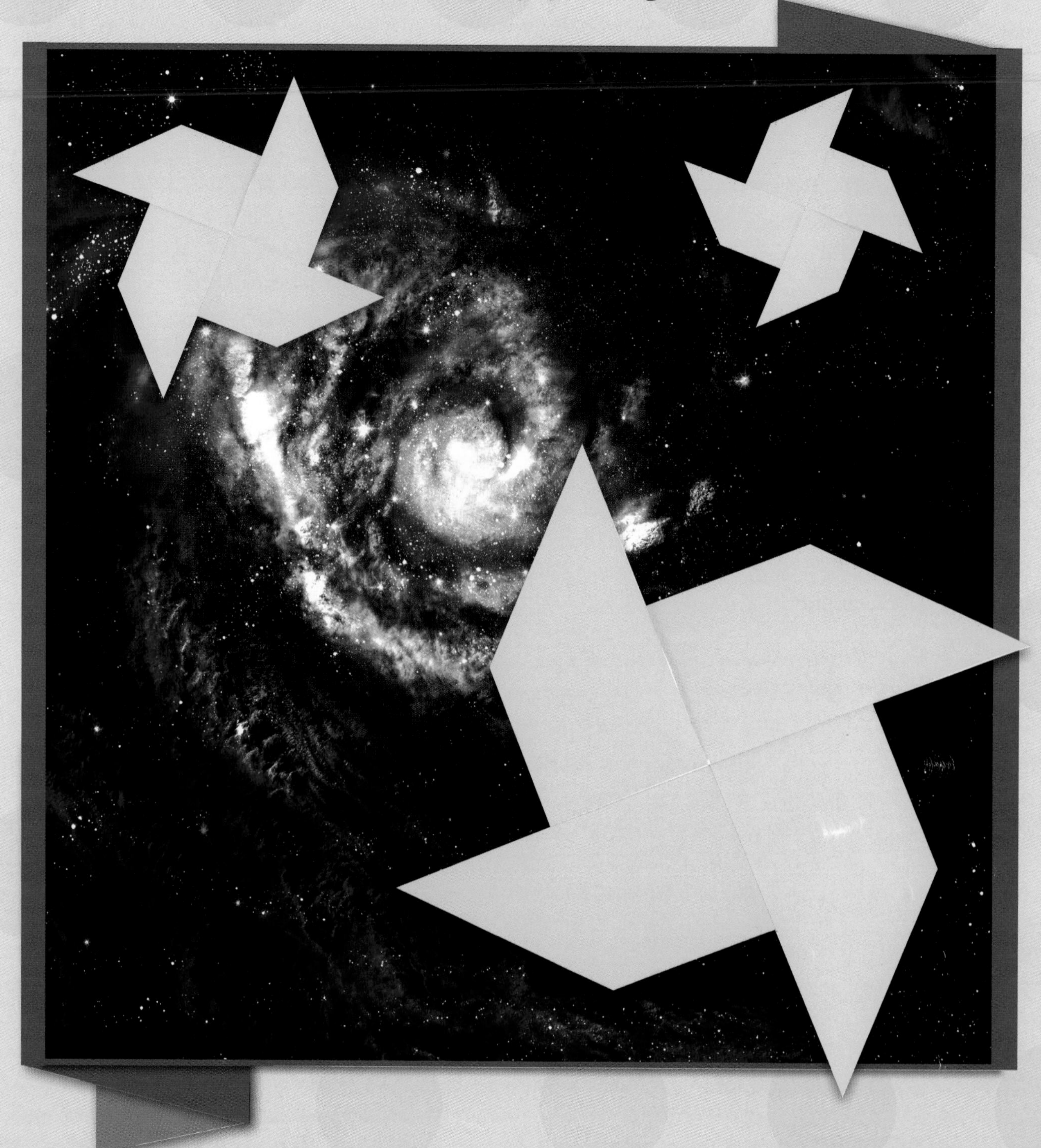

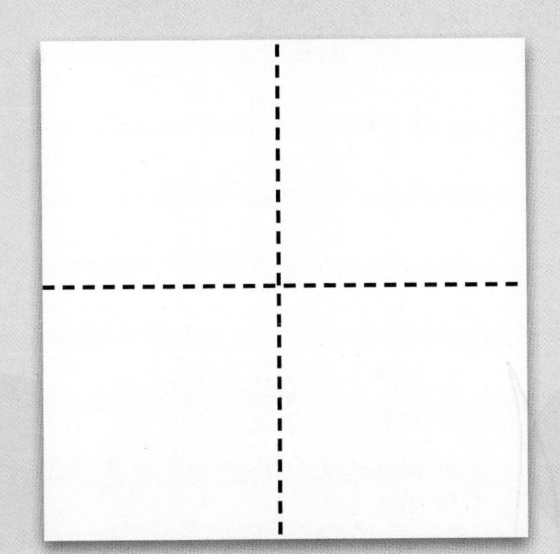

1 Place the paper as shown and fold it in half from top to bottom and unfold, then from left to right and unfold.

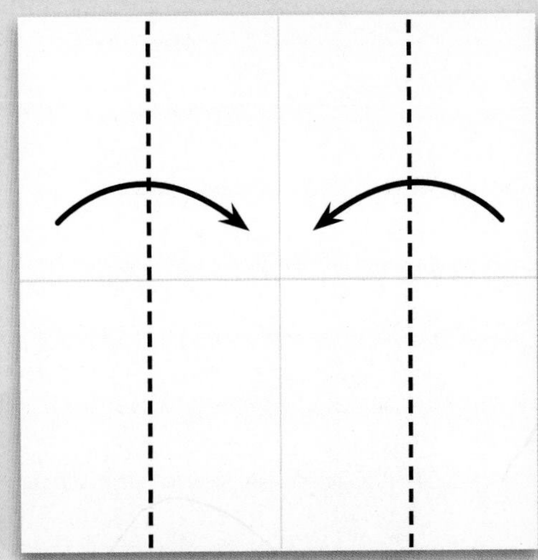

2 Valley fold the sides to meet the center crease.

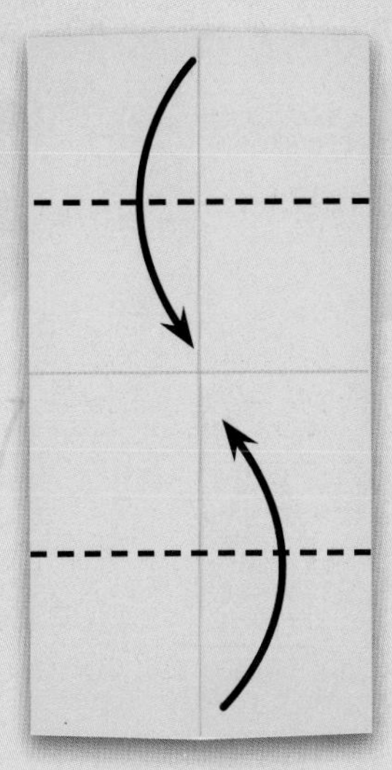

3 Valley fold the top and bottom to meet in the center.

4 Completely unfold the paper.

5 Valley fold the paper diagonally from corner to corner one way and unfold, then from corner to corner the other way and unfold.

Did You Know?

Earth, the sun, and all of the planets in our solar system sit inside a galaxy called the Milky Way. It contains up to 400 billion stars!

6. *Your paper should look like this.*

7. *Pinch the top right corner and fold in the top and the right side along the creases. Flatten the paper.*

8. *Pull out the top left corner, then fold in the left side. Flatten the paper.*

9 Your paper should look like this. Turn the paper upside down.

10 Pull out the top right corner and fold down the top edge.

11 Unfold the top left corner and pull out the point. Fold down the top edge and flatten the model into shape.

12 Your spiral galaxy is ready to spin through space!

Alien

Some people believe that there are strange creatures living in space. Prepare for some out-of-this-world origami when you fold this spooky alien face!

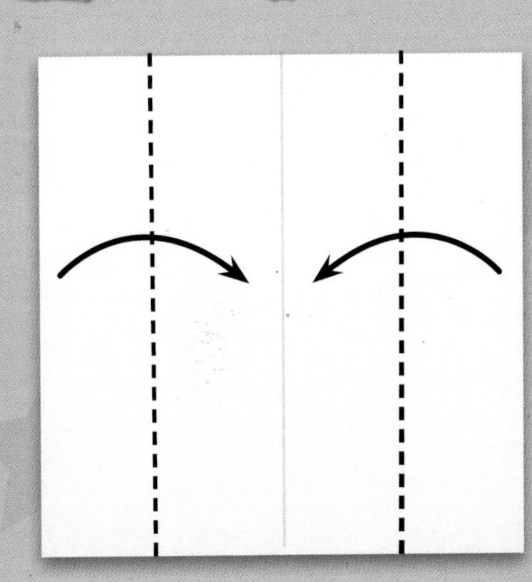

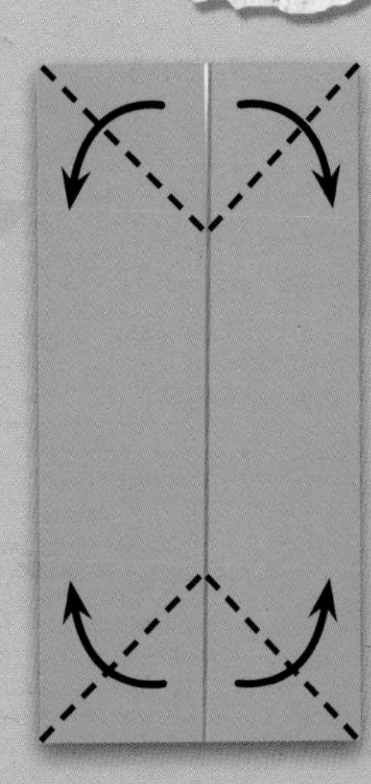

1 Start with the colored side facing down. Fold the paper in half from left to right and unfold.

2 Valley fold the sides to meet the center crease.

3 Valley fold the inner points to meet the outside edges.

4 Valley fold the top right corner and unfold again.

5 Open up the flap and push the corner point over to meet the center crease. Flatten the paper.

6 Repeat steps 4 and 5 on the other side. The white triangles are the alien's eyes.

7 Mountain fold the point at the top.

8 Valley fold the white section.

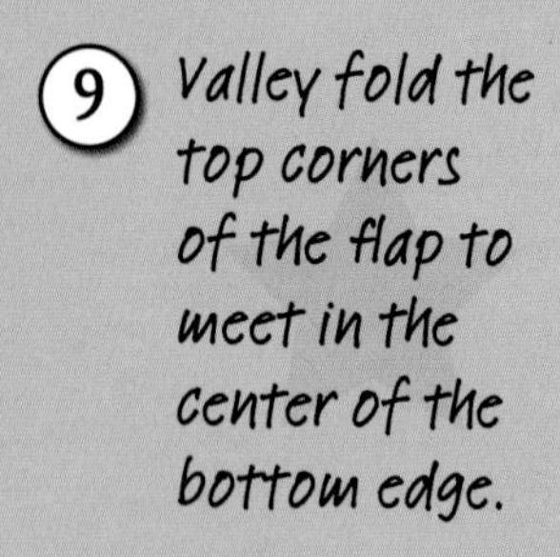

9 Valley fold the top corners of the flap to meet in the center of the bottom edge.

10 Valley fold the inner points to meet the white edges.

Did You Know?

3.6 billion years ago there was fresh water on Mars, which could have been home to microscopic life!

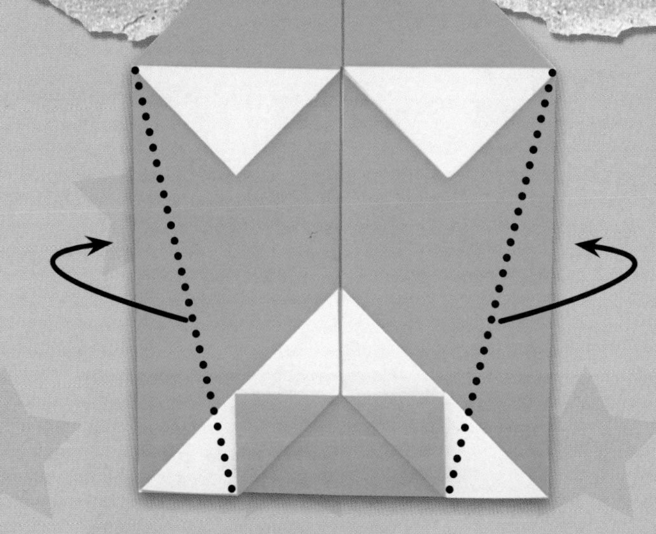

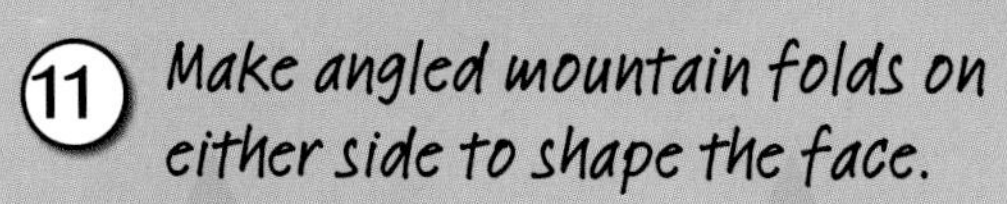

11 Make angled mountain folds on either side to shape the face.

12 Fold down the white triangle.

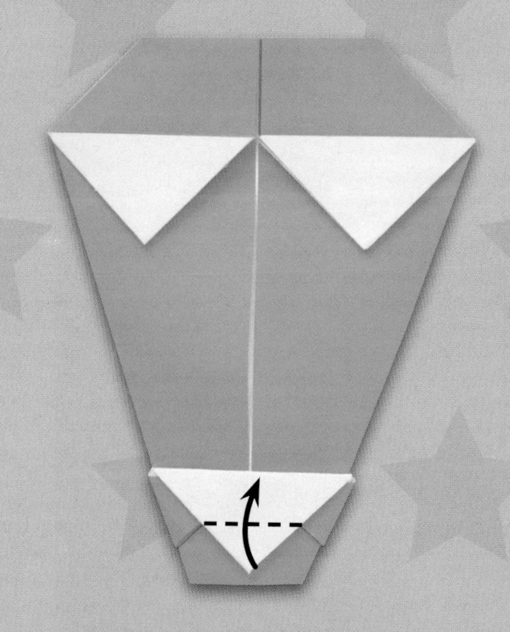

13 Fold the tip of the triangle up. This is the alien's jaw.

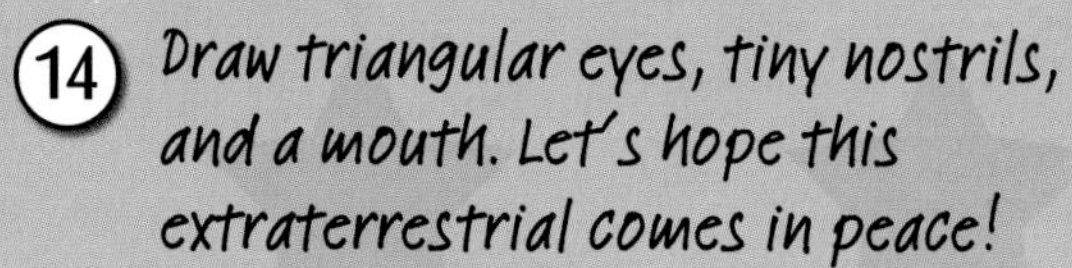

14 Draw triangular eyes, tiny nostrils, and a mouth. Let's hope this extraterrestrial comes in peace!

Space Shuttle

It took a lot of time, money and a team of top scientists to send this awesome, reusable spacecraft into orbit. You can launch a space shuttle in a matter of minutes with a few cosmic folds!

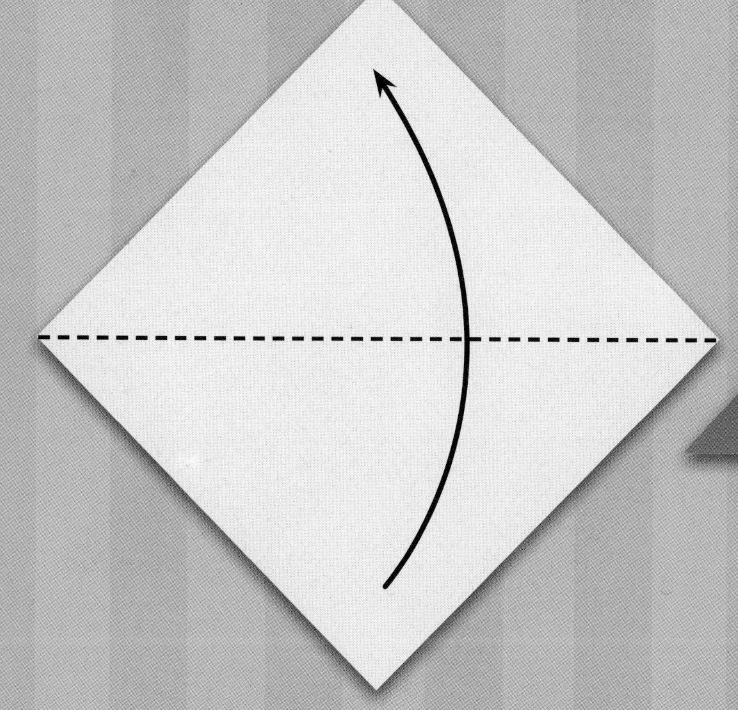

2 Valley fold the right point to meet the top point.

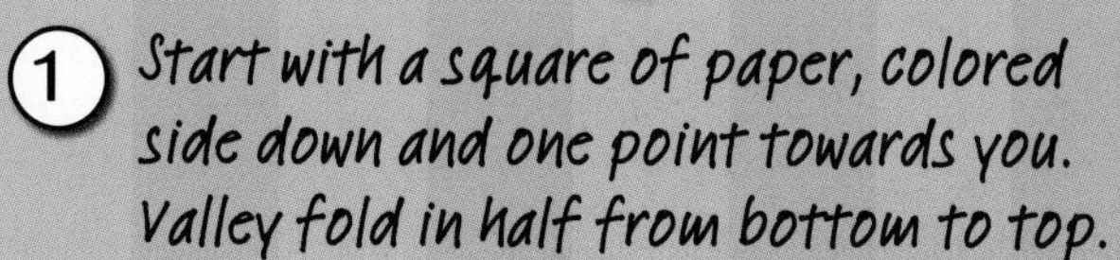

1 Start with a square of paper, colored side down and one point towards you. Valley fold in half from bottom to top.

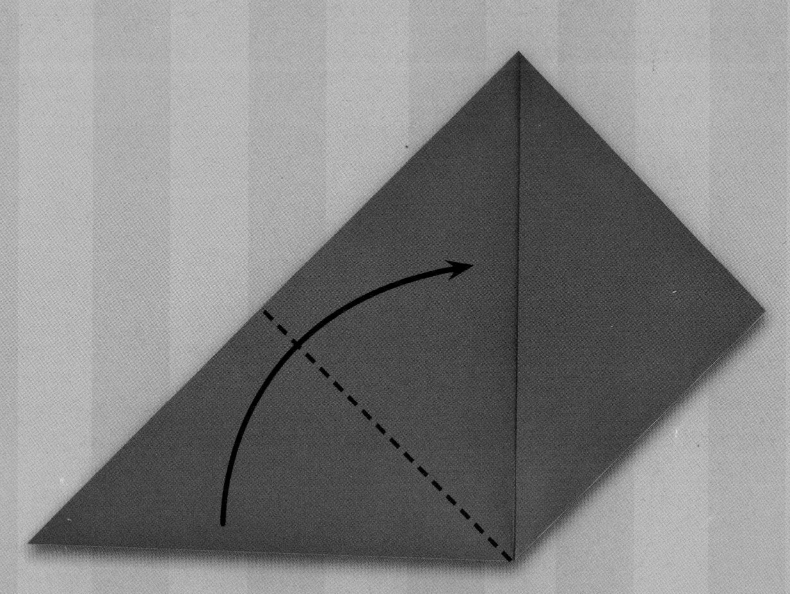

3 Valley fold the left point to meet the top point. This makes a square.

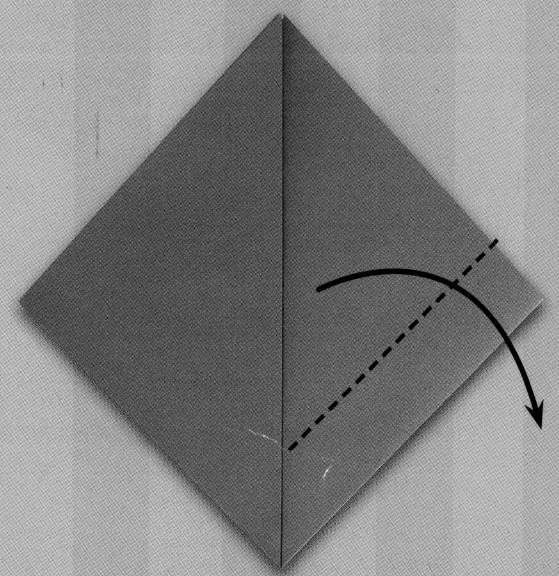

4 Make a valley fold on the right flap about 1/2 inch (15 mm) from the bottom edge.

Did You Know?

While in orbit, the space shuttle traveled around Earth at a speed of about 17,500 mph (28,000 km/h)!

5 *Now make a matching fold on the left flap.*

6 *Valley fold the paper in half from right to left.*

7 *The top point will become the tail. Valley fold the tail to meet the bottom point.*

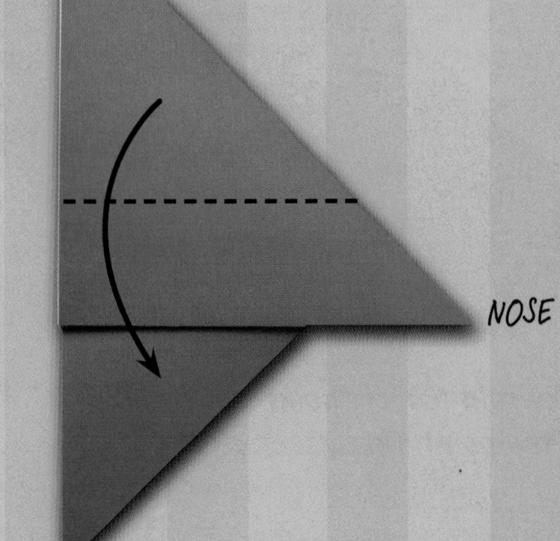

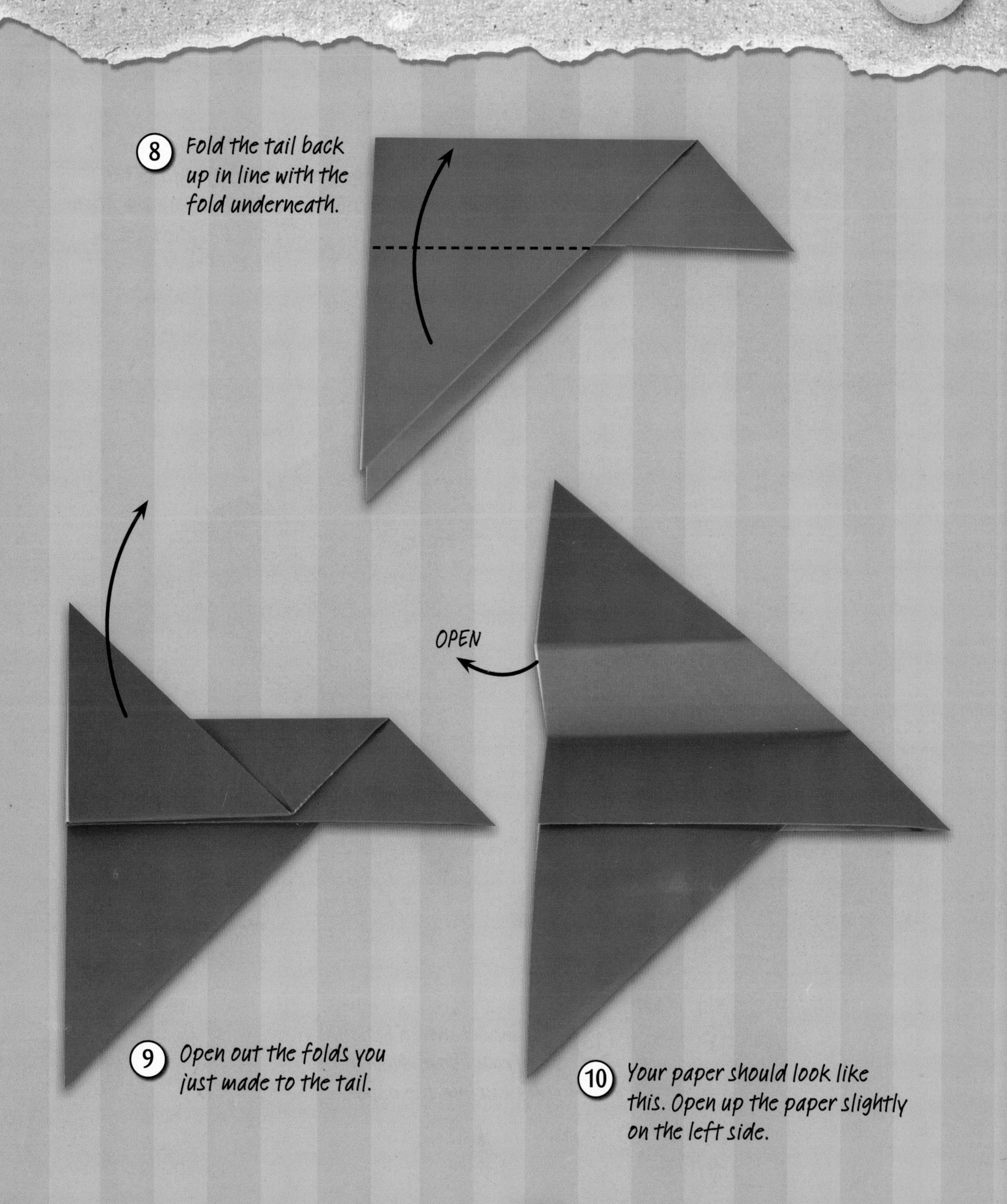
8 Fold the tail back up in line with the fold underneath.
OPEN
9 Open out the folds you just made to the tail.
10 Your paper should look like this. Open up the paper slightly on the left side.

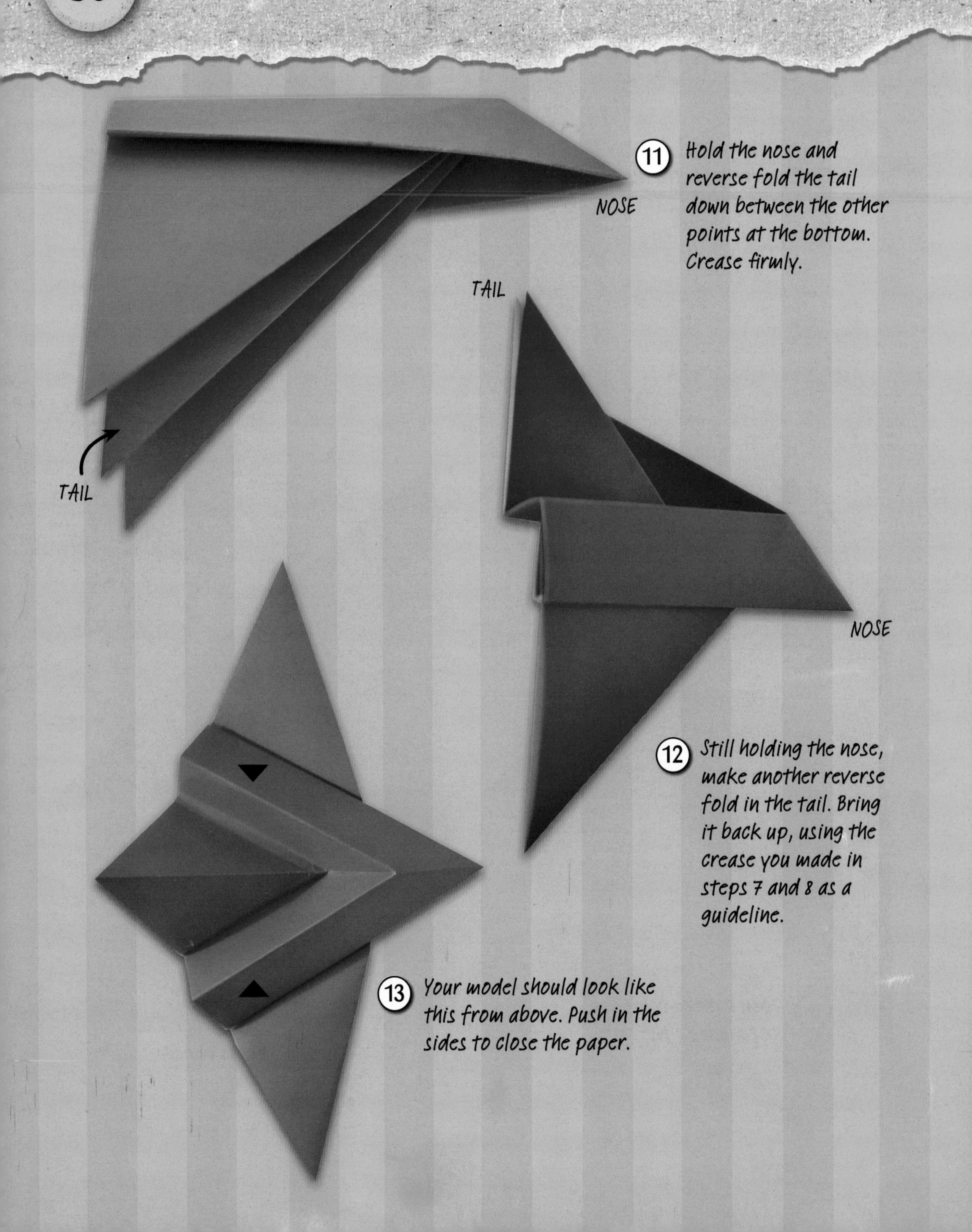

11. Hold the nose and reverse fold the tail down between the other points at the bottom. Crease firmly.

12. Still holding the nose, make another reverse fold in the tail. Bring it back up, using the crease you made in steps 7 and 8 as a guideline.

13. Your model should look like this from above. Push in the sides to close the paper.

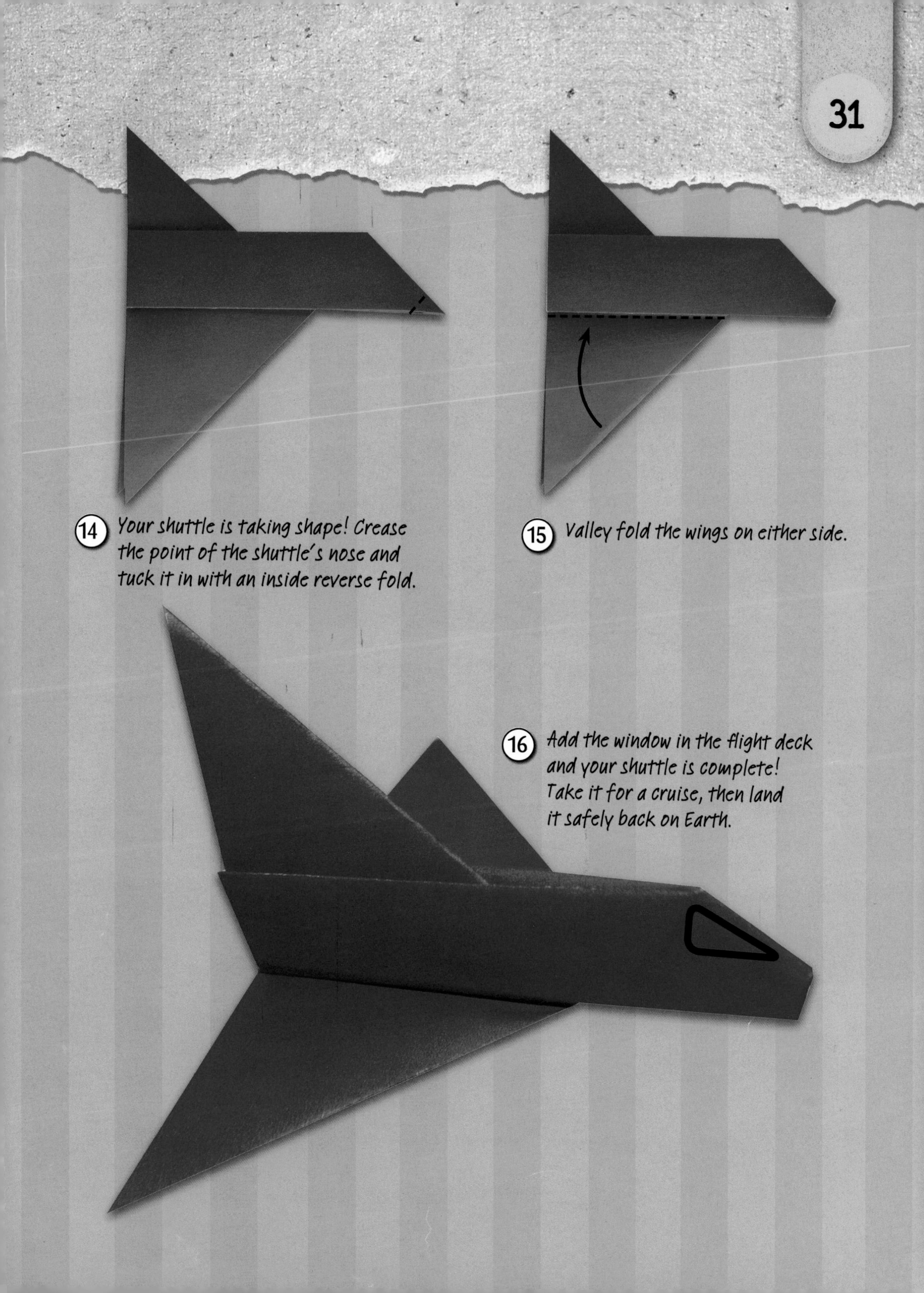

14 Your shuttle is taking shape! Crease the point of the shuttle's nose and tuck it in with an inside reverse fold.

15 Valley fold the wings on either side.

16 Add the window in the flight deck and your shuttle is complete! Take it for a cruise, then land it safely back on Earth.

Glossary

astronauts People who have been trained to travel in a spacecraft.

crease A line in a piece of paper made by folding.

extraterrestrial Something which comes from beyond planet Earth.

International Space Station A large satellite with people on board. It is used by astronauts from many countries to carry out research.

microscopic Very small and only able to be seen with a microscope.

mountain fold An origami step where a piece of paper is folded so that the crease is pointing upwards, like a mountain.

orbit The curved path through which objects in space move around a planet or star.

solar system The sun and the group of eight planets that move around it.

step fold A mountain fold and valley fold next to each other.

UFO (unidentified flying object) A mysterious object seen in the sky that is thought by some people to be from another planet.

valley fold An origami step where a piece of paper is folded so that the crease is pointing downwards, like a valley.

Further Reading

Akass, Susan. *My First Origami Book*. Cico Kidz, 2011.

Biddle, Steve & Megumi Biddle. *Paper Capers*. Dover Publications, 2014.

Ono, Mari & Hiroaki Takai. *Dinogami*. Cico Books, 2012.

Robinson, Nick & Susan Behar. *Origami XOXO*. Ivy Press, 2012.

Index